ALSO BY JOHN AMEN

Poetry Collections

Christening the Dancer
More of Me Disappears
At the Threshold of Alchemy
strange theater
Illusion of an Overwhelm

Collaborations

The New Arcana (with Daniel Y. Harris)

Music

All I'll Never Need
Ridiculous Empire

Dark Souvenirs

Poems by

John Amen

The New York Quarterly Foundation, Inc.
Beacon, New York

NYQ Books™ is an imprint of The New York Quarterly Foundation, Inc.

The New York Quarterly Foundation, Inc.
P. O. Box 470
Beacon, NY 12508

www.nyq.org

First Edition

Set in New Baskerville

Layout and Design by Raymond P. Hammond

Cover Design and Layout: Thia Powers Design

Author Photograph by Chad Weedon

Library of Congress Control Number: 2023952138

ISBN: 978-1-63045-108-0

Dark Souvenirs

CONTENTS

For Richard Sassoon

"I will grow older and I will, it will, something"
—Sarah Kane

"The soul knows no home in the modern cosmos."
—Richard Tarnas

"Then is it sin
To rush into the secret house of death,
Ere death dare come to us?"
—Shakespeare

Family Systems

Three weeks after his bullseye shot,
his cellphone kept dialing—long,
blank messages, I could almost hear
the engine of his breath. He should've
been the world's youngest maestro
but spent his years hiding in the valves
of a westside trumpet, blowing sparks
but no music, a part he couldn't conjure
once he inhaled. Finally I answered,
waited for the caller to begin his confession.
Hope can nail your feet to a burning floor,
grief can smoke the dirt under your shoes.
A month after my brother's funeral—
spackled sky, red blooms on the gardenia—
I could hear my father grinding his teeth
from across the room. My mother stared
out a window, whispering to herself,
deciphering omens in the birdsong.
I told you a thousand times, she blurted,
crazy dervish spinning in my direction,
never hang a hat on a black doorknob.
Now look, just look what you've done.

Relapse

If you had to sit in a windowless room,
processing fingerprints from 7 to 7,
you'd want some action too.
You'd dream of seducing a superhero
outside the Salad Express.
Not that Monday was exotic.
Not that anyone with clout was dreaming of waterlilies.
I signed up for the raffle.
I needed new shoes, especially for the fire drill.
See, I've always been a pragmatist.
The wolf said *we should go somewhere cold,*
he packed the Subaru & drove us north,
hitting the flask at every ramp.
Get used to being thirsty the bear said.
Get used to having blood on your hands the wolf said.
From Levine's open mic to Shaquilla's kitchen,
I've seen drama, buddy, & these distractions don't work with me.
You're talking to someone who regards
bills & newspapers as vaudevillian props.
I was there when the Camco ice machine
spit fire during Belladonna's happy hour.
I recall the '09 citywide spike in psychotherapy,
that feverish crowd marching into the sea.
I saw a champagne cork take out a planet.
I saw basic math dissolve
on the slippery slope of "1 final blowout."
I know how it feels for Jupiter's vacuum
to sweep through your plans.
Keep slamming the junksites & Kentucky blue,
you'll find a Chippendale on Cooper's Berm,
I left a cigarette smoldering in a cereal bowl,
the latest issue of *Fanfare* open to my favorite page.
I know you'll make it when the frost clears.
You'll be the last one off that train,
the morning shakes from Baltimore.

Dark Souvenirs

I studied your craft,
how you drove the demon of gluttonous age
from its hiding place,
freeing the infant who starved for 84 years,
pang & its host
dismantled with a single twitch.
Little mess, little clean-up,
nailbrush, toothbrush, soapy sponge.
No mention in the real-estate ad,
the previous owner's
impeccable marksmanship.
No way to preserve your opus,
air that still trembles,
trying to catch its breath.
Memory does its best
to salvage a keepsake
—pulp, bullet, bone,
a new constellation in the night sky—
but symbols are lost,
art fails, except as it screams at the dead.
I hope what remains of you
can recognize my voice.

Toward a Genealogy

My grandparents,
who sailed to New York in '38,
rarely spoke of the two siblings
who arrived ten years later,
who in every photo I've seen
shrouded the ink on their forearms,
as if to hide it would be enough
to earn the world's forgiveness.
Vi, who moved to Chicago & spent her days
smoking Camels, staring at Lake Michigan
through a seventh-story window.
Alfred, who shredded his money in Texas,
oil that never seeped,
pump that died mid-thrust.
It's easy to forget that breath has wings,
beauty is horror's common-law bride.
Such gospels are understood at dusk,
viewed from over your shoulder
as the sidewalk ends, your lead leg
sinking in the mud.
There are questions I never posed,
& now there's no one to ask,
that line of Jews reborn in America,
my American Jews
buried in Christian ground,
gathered beneath the shadow of a hulking cross,
refugees to the grave
& beyond.

Regrets

I snatched the bottle from his hand
three weeks before he bought the gun.
I quartered the pills
& sponged the dust from his shutters.
I read him headlines
as he smoked cigarettes in the doorway.
Then I drove the Jeep as far as I could
until the gravel turned to dynamite.
He left me his demos,
wine-stained tablature,
family bible, chocolate streaked across its cover.
As the trigger finger follows
the loud voice's lead,
so grief's a flood,
your fists hold back water
for only so long.
Then you're sleeping with the copperheads,
modulating between silos,
waking with your lips on fire.
All summer I've wandered the heroin streets,
visiting every pawnshop in town,
hoping to reclaim that hand-me-down horn
he hadn't played in years.

Two Years

Lingering June, you
strummed your guitar by the mulch pile.
Countdown, Luna moths in the kitchen,
thirty grooves carved in the dining room table.
I was leaving, first day of July,
you stood on the porch,
lit your cigarette & winked.
Summer's burning, I wanted to say,
the Monarchs haven't come home yet.
Listen! The saxes are playing on 13th Street.
I should've rolled down the window,
yelled your name, I didn't, I slammed a gate,
jabbing thread through my lips,
speeding into the stories that came next:
gunshot that no one heard,
absence stamped into indelible print,
three bloodstains on a cushion.
Before I could release the clutch,
the dogwoods were bare, ice in the birdbaths,
two years gone like a skid on the highway,
sky & sky like an empty plate.
I should've tried harder.

Legacy

We spent the summer
playing whiffle ball in the old potter's field.
Every few days, a father set the weeds on fire,
fathers who used a loud voice & stony hands
to teach you the value of gratitude.
For bases & home plate,
we gathered broken birds & sharp objects,
filler that smelled bad & drew blood.
We played late, the oaks
heavy with starlight, bushes teeming with beaconflies.
One morning we emerged from our shotgun row,
field smoking from the previous night's blaze,
odor of gasoline hovering.
The town griever was dead,
slumped under a maple by the rectory.
I agreed not to tell.
I agreed not to squeal in my sleep.
We pinched the griever's lips,
we pulled his penis out of his pants.
Next day, the corpse was gone,
the field marked off with wire,
cops lined the street,
uniforms pressed, their guns glinting in the sun.
Mr. Edney sang a forbidden song,
Mr. Bishop fell to his knees.
Through August & mid-September,
our parents doused their regrets with blackberry hooch,
long, teetering prayers at the kitchen table.
We waited our turn,
a brooding New Year's & murderous July.
We owned fields & houses & destroyed them,
our children owned fields & houses & destroyed them.
For generations we've said *the fire stops here.*
We say a lot of things.

Homecoming

When I was five,
my mother stood in her heels,
tying the picnic basket.
Pull Johnny she'd say, & I'd hoist it into the elderbud,
that pink goddess singing in the twilight.
Brief time in the branches,
long spell serving the monsters
who breed in the caves of the body.

I tug the sail, wind gusts from Macauley Bay.
Turn the key in the stone Buick, an angel appears with a gallon of gas.
There are numerous ways to weave a myth,
& consider the coffer of tunes plucked from the same 7 notes.

I tear through a mumblepatch
where the old house used to stand,
smell of garlic in a bright kitchen,
a jabberjay beating its wings against a west-facing window.

An old man is a young man
who's learned to drop his shoulders
as he walks through the rain.
My heart's a lagging metronome,
my lungs bob in a manic sea.
Blame, I've learned, is another diamond
that has to be given back to the earth,
left where you found it, white petals
shimmering in the dark.

Arc

Ma'd rave
how a possum fell
from a rotten sycamore
the day she brought you home from St. Bartholomew's.
A bad mark, she'd say, *in the Book of Vengeance.*
When I revisit the forced rhymes of our magnolia days,
I'm leveled by lies, hate-storm,
barbed couplets piled in a shallow grave.
I see her in dreams: Ma scattering
possum bones in the ivy, declaring our father dead.
There are rooms I never leave
no matter how far I wander.
Decades & still that mockingbird in the dusk
moans until my heart is stupefied.
When I put that gun to my temple,
I was playing.
You weren't.

First Date

for Stefan, 1971

Like bombwork, my father
wrapped me in his American flag,
filibuster of scissors & comb, blond locks
scattered on faux tile, I died a day.
Clean-cut, square, Ralphie's Grill,
I spun the noodles in the belly of the spoon,
JoAnne pounded the ketchup,
we danced a Neapolitan shake.
Galaxies from the world of hairstyle & menus,
war unfolded, the politician's origami.
Cousins returned, itching their rips & crooked creases.
I took a deep breath, pulled the pin,
lobbed an *I love you.* A kid,
you suck the cold spoon, giggle
over a brain-freeze, wait for your valentine
to toss that beautiful grenade
back in your direction. Later you learn
to nail a punchline while chewing a jackknife,
obey orders, disobey orders, lie awake
burning ancient temples in the dark
—don't misunderstand me, I'm not
giving you a story, I'm trying to work
my way out of one.

Days of Love & Horses

That Memorial Day when I was nine,
the demon leapt from my father's hands.
My wax-paper mom crumpled in the kitchen,
surrounded by coffee mugs. All June & July,
trailers, U-hauls, our house was gaveled
into smoky embers. I kept flying Emily, though,
my Morgan with the milky left eye, surging
above the hospital, courthouse, labor camp.
          These days I rarely see a horse,
but that smoldering August
before the glow turned to ash,
I found myself lost in Scriven's Holler,
toeing those dinosaur traps in the jimsonburr.
Emily carried me through Jones's Gulley,
past the gray & yellow farms, night crashed
as we reached the dilapidated barn.
          Years later, May '99, IC unit on the Oconocluftee,
I grabbed for rocks, branches, craving subsided.
Sprawled on a grassy bank,
I dialed three exes, apologized
for stampeding through their sober lives.
A friend had warned me not to expect *sorrys* in return.
Good thing, I didn't get any.
          Recently in a restless dream, I beheld
that familiar kitchen. My wife hummed the national anthem,
frying slabs of meat in a Mississippi wok. I crawled the floor,
gathering the coffee mugs, & woke to the canter of rain.
          I haven't climbed a saddle in decades,
but when sleep eludes me, skull
throbbing with twisted math & phantom schemes,
I pretend I'm atop my loyal Emily,
we're stranded in a minefield, blind beneath moonless sky.
I squeeze my thighs against her mahogany loins,

bury my face in her mane.
The champing in my belly calms, dawn returns,
the jumps I need to clear don't seem as insurmountable
as when the world is smothered in darkness.
We make it home again, with light to spare.

After Your Memorial
July 2017

You rang my doorbell, I pretended
I wasn't at home, crouched in stillness,
surrounded by photographs—*I should've known,*
I couldn't've known, I should've known—
my neighbor drunk-flashing his porch lights
after his shift at the meat plant, shift at the bar,
his work shirt flung into the azaleas.
Monday, you returned. Tuesday, again.
Wednesday, I answered, that revolving dream,
a disconnect when it mattered most, your fist
frozen mid-knock. I held your trumpet toward you,
kissing the haze between worlds, I uncoiled
on the front steps beside the wisteria,
cool air swirling into the yard as you fled
through tall grass, past the rhododendrons,
this green life you'd already forgotten.

Haunted

Sir frontman, Mr. minstrel,
we smoked your tablature
on the clover berm by I-51.
Now your jazz is woven into the American nest,
blooming in roadkill. Home,
I sprinkled a sax solo
in the backyard where you
blared that blood lake, sulfur cloud,
where black tomatoes crescendo, bitter squash,
those gunpowder peaches.
Four Julys come & gone,
August bursting with a jackpot I can't give away,
& that bulletweed, no matter
how I dig & pull, it comes back,
redder & louder every time.

To Find You Like That

The angel asked if you were ready to go,
& you said that you wanted to stay a bit longer
with the red lilies in the rock garden.
You wanted to play your horn in the bleeding petals,
in the long, hairy vines,
you wanted to wait & see
if anyone would show up to delay your performance.
It's time, the angel said, impatient
as you paced a straight line back & forth
by the red lilies in the rock garden.
& that's where I found you in the morning,
after coffee & newspapers,
after I'd convinced myself I was worthless,
I'd convinced myself I was a god,
to walk into the red lilies in the rock garden
& find you like that,
fuck to find you like that.

Defiance

You writhed on the gurney as Dr. V
slipped his forceps past your tonsils,
the word *more* lodged in your windpipe.
Years later, trumpet in one hand,
strap in the other, you
drilled a solo, drilled a needle, solo, needle,
until the needle won,
bebop flooded in that milky dream.
Hence, my joke: look up the word *addict,*
your glossy mug thrumming on the page.

There's a witch—mischievous at best—who always gets a say,
which is why our mother taught us
to set a place for her at the table
lest she show up on her own terms,
wielding all that dust & fire.
Was that the last thing you saw
as you pressed the barrel to your lips, the witch
towering in the corner saying *we could've avoided this?*
& you, who always hoarded the final word,
would rather tug your little trigger
than give her what she wanted.

First Marriage
for David R, 1968

We were married at the courthouse
before I left for the war overseas
—prayer on a felony charge,
seven bags of electric powder.
She had her own battles,
dodging the tripwire in her skull,
pill vials lined up like grenades.
When I returned, my heart
plastic-wrapped, stashed in a duffel bag,
I tore apart the house,
found a sharp melody under a pair of shorts,
a flat guitar riff in my sock drawer.
Our song crumbled in the dim light,
even desire, that soaring hook,
failed to reel us in.
She buried her meds in the backyard.
I spent hours by the door, listening for footsteps.
Saint Patty's, I waved from our living room
as she boarded a spaceship docked in the kitchen.
She took the bed.
I kept the Teflon pans.
That was fifty years ago, man,
that was yesterday.

Understanding

in the spring

I wasn't going to do it, just wanted to pick up
that suicide scent, memorize the urge. I gripped
his pistol, I wasn't going to do it, believe me,
just needed to catch the feeling, slip the brass
into the cartridge, smooth as lubricated flesh,
my teeth clicking on the barrel. A white stupor
splashed over me—his auroral Gethsemane,
that extraordinary, that irrevocable twitch—
I couldn't master the trigger, couldn't finish
my ritual. I spilled the bullets on the rug, fled
into my yard, ripe with blossoms & birdsong,
two or three times whispered *I'm sorry I'm sorry,*
I don't know for what or to whom I was speaking.

Foster

Black Richard & pale I spent our sugar years
stomping through woods in search of a devil.
Our sisters swapped confessions on the wraparound porch.
Sometimes at the tack shop
a tourist unfolded his map,
told us of horned beasts & forty nights in a desert.
He slipped us candy & cash
when no one was looking.
We rode that high,
frothed with new ambition,
idling in the riverbed, those
bellyfuls of stammer wine.
By the goat sty, money ma clutched her switch,
dollar da snapped his belt, they'd
line us up & count their wards, deciding
who was the favorite of the day.
Six kids perfecting their bluff, gamblers praying
they could beat the odds.

Breathless

Richard rented a Corolla, blitzed the highway
from Brooklyn to Beaufort. A week in the orchard,
tripping among the apple trees, we rocketed to the coast.
He ignored the lifeguard's whistle,
splashing with great whites & killer whales.
I read on the beach, Richard swam.
I read *War & Peace,* he staggered in the hot sand,
gasping as I finished *War & Peace* & started *Don Quixote.*
The sun crawled across the sky & the sky & sky.
Home, he called to say there was a monster thrashing in his stomach.
He said it was our dead parents
carving their initials in his third chakra.
The doctor gave him a bad diagnosis.
His girlfriend Sylvia read to him as he sat in a rocking chair.
They watched reruns on a miniature tv.
When Tricky Dick appeared on the screen, hunched over,
flashing peace signs, he burst out laughing.
He asked me what was going on with the horses.
He asked me if my pages were dry,
if I still cooked chicken paella for the bankers in Argentina.
Then it was June, I was the one with the rental, speeding up 95 at dawn.
I don't recall his funeral as much as dressing for it,
suiting up in his fourth-floor apartment.
No shades, diamond light glared, slicing through dirty glass.
I couldn't find my breath, I was alone,
not for the first time, certainly not the last.
I remember thinking, & now the misgiving returns
as muggy summer pounces, I too am stranded
in dangerous water, no ghost ship swelling on the horizon,
no mermaid gliding from the weedy depths,
I'm the only one who can get me back to the shore.

Poem for Bill B

Bill B & I met & got sober in May '89, hours spent
in musty church basements, smoke-filled VFW halls,
discussions, confessions over pots of black coffee.
I pounded for UPS, carting boxes from ten to six,
slept in a Days Inn by the airport. Someone dropped
a cigarette on a mattress, flames erupted at one AM
on a Monday. By dawn, the street was littered with
charred furniture, damp ash strewn for miles. Mike M
died that year in a car wreck, LJ guzzled a pint after
four months clean, cannon-balled off a rooftop dock.
Cops dragged Lanier for a week, never found his body.
My brother's first son shouldered his way into the light.
Elizabeth R married Stephane B, white gowns, tuxes,
bagpipes in the afternoon. Tumors swung through
my girlfriend Rhonda's intestines, liver. I was bellowing
into a microphone when she passed, stomping a distortion
pedal in a club near Richmond. After her funeral, I
stashed my Strat, landed back in the classrooms, treading
those German philosophers, all that volition & angst.
Bill went off his meds, crashed in a Meck County unit:
ECT, a dozen pills in a paper cup, venting to therapists
until his throat was raw. One Sunday in the cafeteria,
we couldn't keep the conversation propped. Fatigue rattled
the table like a foreshock, steel beams & concrete pads
dropping from the heights. The world fell apart for a while.
Today I thought of Bill, wondered if he was alive.
I searched his name, the local obits. I felt that alien ship
hovering above the powerlines, the same way I did when
my younger sister died. Buddhists talk of impermanence,
how all content dissolves, what you've acquired, people
you love, consciousness itself. I know I cling too firmly
to my wife, as if we're huddled on a pontoon in a swollen sea,
drifting toward a sudden edge. Some nights, the earth
is indeed flat, all currents heaving toward that bottomless
drop-off, the tumble of oblivion. Summer lingers, there's

a song I've wanted to write since I was a kid, I can't nail
the chords. A wild melody swirls in my head, I can't
translate it, can't seem to access that ancient ship buzzing
in the clouds, ladders swinging all around me. Bill was
Catholic, I was agnostic. He prayed to his Christ, I listened
for the echo. But some days I long to believe those tales
of a golden afterlife, the purging of consternation, how we
might behold ourselves differently. Though perhaps we
ignored the angels during our terrestrial stay, we might
in that balmy glow, free of craving, heed their patient call.

The 80s

At first, the beast had no name.
Then we muttered that acronym,
as if by speaking the unspeakable
we might explode in our shoes.
My friend's sister died in her aunt's guest room,
skin bruised, an ancient child with a shrinking memory.
New wave sparked in the eastside clubs,
a bartender named Richard dove from the Brooklyn Bridge.
Crucify them! the preacher said.
Lock them up! the protester said.
Millions reduced to ash, a tireless enemy
flitting from blood to blood, corpses
& corpses in that sinister game of tag.
I fluffed my backpack, descending the steepest stairs I've known,
so many handprints on the banister,
bus tires pounding a cocaine dream.
I'll never go back, I said. By the time I reconsidered,
I looked like the glowering strangers
in those shoe-box photos, relatives whose names
were scrawled in Mom's worn bible.
Hello Hudson, hello East River, hello Joralemon Street.
Every door I slammed I had to reopen,
miming letters to the deceased,
burning them in parks, at busy intersections.
& while that strobe of cherubs mostly moved on
to wherever cherubs finally go, a few
still linger. They track the new flood
as it swells in the dark, bracing for its arrival.

Local News

The Friday Isabel's father went missing,
he flashed a knife in a downtown bar,
fired his 45 into his ex's apartment,
screaming threats at 4 am in a cul-de-sac.
When the cops arrived,
he & his green Malibu were gone.
At dawn, they converged on his house,
wielding crowbars & a battering ram,
roped off shelves of porn, boxes of ammo,
a mannequin stuffed in a strait jacket,
another wrapped in chains, he'd drawn
teardrops on their cheeks
& smeared their mouths with paint.
I kept seeing him in our backyard,
unshaven face grinning in the branches.
He pressed his lips against my windowpane.
Once he sat next to me
at the Pavilion movie theater,
running his fingertips over my zipper.
Isabel sealed her family photos in a baggie,
we buried them in the woods,
she tore branches from the pines
& dragged thorns across her flesh
as any child of Tartarus would.
Weeks later, leaves turning, half-
moon hanging, I dug up the evidence,
that flare of shame behind the schoolhouse.
I pissed & pissed,
the longest piss of my life,
I was like a fireman who keeps spraying a house
hours after the flames have surrendered,
wanting to be sure,
convinced the embers are playing dead,
he can hear a spark
whispering in all that wreckage.

Recovery

A hand stretches from deep space
& taps you on the shoulder.
You've been through this routine
enough times that you no longer turn.
You reach forward, into hard light & bells.
This is it, centerstage in Shangri-Blah,
your confession offered to the books.
You elbow someone whom you vaguely recognize.
He offers to modify his routine.
He offers to perform the wedding.
You stand on the deck of the Mother Louise,
your return voyage through manic straits,
watching the hull carve through waves,
thinking you've revised the print,
you're a new man with a new karma.
But causality dissolves at this point,
each scenario occurs in a different room,
even if all take place in a single beachfront tower
fated for demolition. Goodbye passport office.
Goodbye Department of Romantic Processes.
Department of the Death Wish.
Who you were can never meet who you are
can never meet who you'll be.
In any case, horns should be blowing.
This is galactic jazz, big-bang sexy.
You've always liked the idea
that something larger, broader plays you
like an oboe, squeezing out your
golden notes, an exotic scale worthy of primetime.
Here's your defining moment, & this time
you get the joke: there's no way to take credit.
Don't be surprised if you feel relieved.
The Department of Regrets has closed.
The Department of Egoic Affairs has downsized.
Even the Department of Transcendent Concerns

has reduced its hours. Soon: that flurry
of hammers, boarded panes, the clustering
void & lull of atoms. Ancient solitude,
now your real work can begin.

Addict

Blind harpy, rapids in your vein,
heart that stutters behind the strapping dusk.
Gospel of amnesia,
gospel of recollection.
It's worth flushing
every schoolhouse in your kingdom
to walk the gauntlet of that ill-lit paradise
one more time,
one more time,
one more time,
nodding a confession
as you devour the sins of the world.

Ode to Country Music

after Sparklehorse

I come from men who shoveled reserve for a living.
Who needs the wings of communion?
The veindrain of forgiveness?
Last night, my drowned brother paused at the fence,
parted his lips to sing, then vanished,
a shy oracle leaving a trail of mud
in the yellow leaves. The world
has always been broken or breaking,
& who can say whether loss or contentment
is the heart's lifeblood. Who can say
whether time is bored or ambitious. Who's
beyond reloading, firing a prayer into the long night?

Where the Work Is

Thirteen sleeps until I see you again,
that's the lie I told myself,
& how easily a prayer became a demand,
the phone blustered in the empty house,
smoke billowed with each ring.
You never finished what you were saying
before the line exploded, no way
to strap the bullet to its wired seat,
drive oily death back to his casino town.
Now your absence is my outpost,
bunker where I've spent half a year
scrubbing three bloodstains, cobbling
a juju from specks of metal, specks of bone.
Truth is, I don't know how to wait,
that's where the work is.

What I Remember

My skin sprouted the devil's fur.
Each night, ma's ripe orgasm
poured like sugar juice over my dreams.
I wrestled my trumpet as across the brickfield,
Smithy towered waist-deep in the river,
firing his rifle into the banks.
I lived on the sweet pulp of my anger,
though every peach I picked came back to haunt me,
ma spread naked on a bare mattress,
her hand vised between her legs.
I gargled black sap as developers streamed in,
their dollars strewn across our graves.
I looked for God in a bubbling spoon,
as if the next jab might peel my memory,
unstrap me at the door of forgiveness.
I played my trumpet as a bulldozer
rolled over the peach trees, I played it when ma
drowned in her bathtub, when the preacher
said the world would end on a Thursday.
A week before Christmas '08, I set it down in the culvert
behind the new condominiums where our shed
used to stand, those red saws & pitchforks,
the teeth & tines of my longing,
I haven't thought of playing it since.

Multiverse

He woke in a bad place, straddling
the downtown 6 past the haunted Ferris wheel,
whiplash at the clinic north of Liar's Canyon.
He didn't harass the driver, didn't
crowbar the rules, he nodded in his seat,
cheek flattened against the window, miles
of concrete & fire, crime tape flapping between the trees.
He taped quarters to his eyes,
tucked a king of spades in his lapel pocket.
His wife took the circle express,
snatched a black coffee at Mac's bodega.
Electricity flickered, she screamed in the hallway,
a vase of tulips shattered on the marble floor.
She spent nights steering the violent city blocks in a convertible.
She saw him or an actor who looked like him chasing the Local 12,
she didn't see him again, the buses stopped running,
Jabber Heights overflowed with mattresses & plastic,
a tent village blossomed like a lotus.
She sold the convertible, he trembled
along the dead route, shaking the storefronts.
First day of July, a police officer knocked on her door.
She knew what he was going to tell her,
she could hear his breath, she could feel his ear
pressed against the keyhole.

The 49 Days

*

Alone & hungry, I woke,
Sylvia's hands slid across the keyboard,
she & her students hunched over a blue Steinway.
Moments later they vanished mid-sonata,
the piano gutted in the front yard,
chips of ivory scattered in the mulch.
I called into the closets, couldn't remember names.
I turned, a man with a blank white mask
reached for my shoulder in the yellow afternoon.
Richard? he said, & the name
meant nothing to me.

*

Across the berm, ankle-deep in a puddle of gas,
my brother recited the alphabet. He held
a gold lighter to the sky. I heard the tulip tree
cry to the oak, that electric thread drumming in the subsoil.
The earth swiveled, I was cuffed to a long, black table,
a revolver smoked on a purple tray.
In the thick air ripe with summer,
five naked people stared. *It's me, Richard,
it's me!* each shouted, I had no idea in the muted light,
the now silver room who they were.

*

I'm here! I yelled. My pulse shook the beams,
knocked vases from shelves, Sylvia couldn't taste me,
the play was about to resume. I couldn't exit
that endless intermission, floating in the mezzanine.
An understudy clutched Sylvia's arm,
men in black suits, women in black skirts,
she grumbled as they swept her across the marble.

44

Dialogue thundered, staccato scenes about a mafia town,
a family that played boardgames inside a block of ice, a salesman
from California who swore he could make it rain. Sylvia
closed her eyes for the second act, I reached through a glare,
I couldn't land my touch, I was made of distance.

*

                    The soldier my father posed by the scrap pile
            in a Confederate costume, leaning on a sledgehammer
            as he slurred barbwire jokes. He demanded laughter,
                    I wouldn't give it to him, he looked away first,
            I sparked through pine needles toward the curing shed,
        he prodded again, again my rebuff, that embryonic heresy,
                    we drew our pistols amidst the jumbletrees
                    where how many black bodies were strung.
            Later the drunken giants from concentric hollers
            arrived in rusted cars, rolled their dice in the garage,
                    flung their cards, howling in the crazy star-glow.
            Later he chattered to himself, that gulp of anger,
            & how he wrung his hands, hurling his broken wallet
            into the slug-pond, as if rage were his only inheritance,
        as if it were mine now, as if I had no right to turn it down,
            the fourth Richard, Richard the fourth in a withered line.

*

Sunrise wrapped the walls, the blind kid
swung his ax as morning arrived,
heaving its way up the mountain.
Wireweed crept across the donkey field,
kudzu galloped over the dry valley.
I couldn't saddle my ambitions,
couldn't find my way in the green hall.
I waved my gun, stumbled amongst lamps,

baskets & antique tables, boxes of photos.
Later the piano sounded odd scales, the
brown bench crumbled, tablature wafted
like pigeons on fire, beautiful alien sphere,
limbo swaddled in a morphine blur.

*

My cell rang in the afternoon.
My friend couldn't shake his dream,
sitting across from me in a Sunken City café.
I tried to bring you back, he explained,
his voice disappearing in the ether.
Richard! Richard! he yelled into the phone,
the future fluttered in my throat,
I swallowed a river, my confession bobbing to the surface,
not about the dream but my mother & her obsession with birds,
how she taped feathers to my chest
before I dressed & left for school.
Protection, she said, *from the world's poisonous song.*
We hung up, I hovered in that private smog,
all day stumbled into walls & furniture.
I couldn't locate myself, & I kept
hearing the roar of water, though it hadn't
rained in at least a month.

*

I couldn't speak Sylvia my love, this tongue
made of lead, couldn't translate my afterworld,
gases flaring, icy avalanches in the gloom.
Once you lay beside me, muttering in my ear,
I tasted the heat of your breath.
The soil between your legs was loud,
flood on my thighs,

46

my body the brittle ark
sang through your stormy current.
So much unsaid, word by word
I'm dismantled, not how I meant to cross
this celestial fault line, dashed one tremor to the next,
my final, pulpy work, sprawled on a Chippendale
at eternal noon, shutters drawn, windows black.
Secrets I kept from you Sylvia, myself, now what remain.

*

What foul galleon flew the dock, I perched
a mad gull the razored balustrade.
Then on infinite gangway, then
stretched arms wide to the bow,
I called in spindrift, *wait! wait!*
What dying desire insane to stoke
I tore & stabbed with invisible hands.
& the restless ship, plodding mammoth,
bawled like a dire Sphinx, lunged from the light,
melting as I quivered on the chain.
& the stranger for whom I felt
such rended lust had vanished, I was
sun-wiped, a million stars beyond.

*

I floated in a black hole, gripping a paintbrush,
offered a wild, evaporating stroke to the eidetic air.
It's true what's said about the death-gate flash,
orbits & counter-orbits, gravities jerked & shoved,
that flipbook of faces, then a tunnel, so many shuffling
slack-jawed, carting their self-inflicted wounds.
Thin tethers snapped with each step,
above, around me, voices familiar,

a thrum of planets, I joined the queue
marching through petrified bones, memory
ever-condensing, greed & panic swirled
to produce a love I could never name.
Before even the spatter on the wall,
I knew a circle of grief, beauty as acid & balm,
the life so cursed soon tropical, succulent, sweeter in regret.
I was no longer that boy, that Richard, that ghost,
that wispy form flickering in a bardo.

Ode to Mythology
(the greatest award of them all)
           for Craig

Twenty-one again,
I was responsible for the string parts,
the crescendos, I rolled a mean joint,
stoked a decent improv.
My friend had overdosed a few days before,
I was waiting for a delivery, watching
for that famous lemon hearse.
It was like being an amateur Moses
or playing Mannequin Z
on a nuclear test site.
I pressed my guts to my spine,
determined to sing my part
without coughing on the directory.
Glasses clinked in the background.
Lights flickered, & when I put my
hand to the switch, I entered a movie,
it was like I finally became the actor I was meant to be.
I could feel it, I was about to win
the greatest award of them all.

Usually when I recall you
May 3

You're slumped under a pear tree playing a dented horn.
Sharp phrases steam in the grass, G scale like the moan
of Judas, your mangled A minor wail the death of crows
by thirst. Today I pictured you twirling in the heavy rain,
instrument tucked under your shirt. I'd like to remember
you like that, not yield to what always jangles next, that
staccato blast in the pawnshop, a cop calling at three in the
morning. Did a powder-blue opus mushroom in your skull?
A one-note solo that fired the angels into madness? Did
you lift your eyes to behold a sky filled with red starlings?
But then, music was a language you never mastered, this
poem is simply tableau, psychodrama, a brother baptizing
himself in metaphors, splashing the smoke from his eyes.
This is how a bumpy, blaring day unfolds 2+ years later.

Catherine

for Catherine Rahn-Root

Police divers shovel Lake Forever,
the glassblower & her starfish,
her orange octopus with the severed arms.
Dragged from weedy sand,
hauled to shore in a wire net,
she's surrounded by paramedics,
half gorgon, half mermaid,
crowd gasping as her face softens,
fins & tail retract,
legs sprouting from her torso.
Then she's the most beautiful, the unluckiest
woman ever born, diva flushed with morphine,
belted to a gurney. Diagnosis,
nails of Prozac, Seroquel,
volts drunk-dancing in her brain.
Glue. Collage. Crayons on cardboard.
I talk to the unborn, she tells her doctors,
dashing a stick figure in purple.
Nurses prod with rubber hands,
the sharp edge of dull questions,
psychotropic dreams in the lab.
Clutching her breath for days, she fingerpaints
sailors in the coral, how sunlight pools on black stone.
She waits for something, anything
to break water in the dark.

Ode to Country Music 2

after Big Thief

The man I fought with,
whose ruptured limbs I left by the river,
was gone in the morning.
I saw his face on billboards & wanted posters,
scanned for him as I passed through taped-off fields.
I read about him in newspapers, bibles, the ancient encyclopedia.

I found a map to Biltmore,
kids were shooting bottles
behind the guardhouse,
staring as if they'd
known me in another life.

Those days I slept in dangerous beds,
waiting for the knife in the pillow,
before the waters receded & my cousins reclaimed their land,
before I invented the airplane
& soared west to begin again.

Roman à Clef

Summer days my dad was drunk by dusk,
firing his 12-gauge at the grackles,
those rimy-eyed phantoms whistling in the hemlock.
Later, ma would send me
into the blackness to find him,
lost in Crawford's orchard,
mumbling to himself in the dirt.

I was sixteen when Suzanne the beekeeper
peeled off her spacesuit
on the broad bank of the Pacolet,
a 9mm tattooed on her right breast, a bible on her left.
I spent July & August
worshipping the pistol & the good book,
came to on a slippery rock,
gun-shy & devil-bruised,
when she left for Murphy in September.

I picture my parents as the shadows I knew
when we lived in that rickety house,
the creaky bones, colander roof, staircase
moaning like an out of tune cello:
dad, who died sober a decade ago, pacing in the woods,
ma, whose memory dried like a creek bed,
floating through a blue room with a vacation smile.

Some nights I ride those wings
back to the river & the evergreens,
Suzanne towering in the wet grass,
hands slapping at the moon.
My body flares with the din of the grackles,
their manic jazz, one savage horn rising over the rest.
In dream after dream, it's the music I always wanted,
& before I wake, starlight
spills over me, over everything.

Apprenticeship

My brother & I memorized our parents' epic—their curses & grunts—
mastering that pidgin of volatility. We can feel an earthquake rising
in the slightest twitch of an eyebrow, murder begins with a pinch of
the lips. I swear *brood* has a particular smell, *fester* has a sound, like an
orchestra of snipers tuning in the dark.

Funeral Dream

anniversary

Breaststroke through rooms filled with suits, dresses, cash registers, a Steinway, every black key removed. I found the mortician wrapped in seaweed. He gurgled his résumé, credit cards nailed to his feet, years of betting on bad limbs, bad science. He handed me a silver carving knife, I glided through watery tons, searching, searching for the hero's body. Above us, our guardians took notes, sipping their belladonna martinis.

Pivot
for SH

After is what I remember best, three survivors hunkered over cereal & bread, my mother dodging questions as if they were weak spots in the pinewood floor. Phantom father, in dreams I hover in that second-story window where once I clenched my eyes, praying for you to change your mind, for the lion on the cross to change it for you. I shriek behind glass, your '63 Buick crumbling in the oak trees—then a swarm of silence, swarm of laughter.

Anniversary

Your pistol, dried sunflowers, that unfinished canvas—visions of you wrapped in a gunpowder glare. The living fled, scattering their complaints like babelseed. You stayed behind, howling in the shelves. You couldn't have left if you'd wanted to.

Bardo

for David

I could see my son talking to himself, shadow-boxing his diagnosis. I remember wearing a hat made of smoke. What hurts is I left the ones I love wandering in the leaves, it wasn't entirely by choice, I barely remember that carefree bullet.

At Some Point

You flapped for the sun, the sky held its ground. Rubber light & Oxy dawns. Flash of the barrel, your name powder in the haze, how my own life is divided—the lull before, the lull after.

Vigil

A visit from our mother of blades, dressed in gauze, eyelids smeared with mascara. *Why'd he pull the trigger?* she asked. Remnants of you tethered to a sulfuric cloud, our mother's shrill voice bouncing in the tunnel. I pulled the space blanket tight & prayed over your corpse. New voices instructed me, rising from the glow of September.

Backstory

for SC

—preppers in camouflage marked every door in Dyersville. Ma gathered sugar, life jackets, Mason jars for the brew, some pink hyacinths, a bagful of dirt. We packed our keepsakes. Heirlooms. Jujus. Death wore a tie-dye t-shirt & camouflage pants. He shambled his way to the promenade, busking beside the Ferris wheel. It was all symbolic at that point, as the professor explained. Then the recession began, this is when I fell in love with country music—

Fifteen
Old Town

They made out in the couple's bed, spinning impersonations, Sam's Blackbeard, Jimi's Scarlett O'Hara. Light rain skipped on a metal roof. Jimi found the woman's makeup, a wedding dress bagged in a closet, Sam put on the guy's seersucker jacket. *Be my bride*, he snarled, collapsing to one knee. Jimi's cheeks blushed with rouge, eyelashes dripping black mascara. They poured chips & scooped raspberry sorbet into salad bowls, guzzled mango juice from wine glasses. When they caught a bustle on the porch, key in the lock, they fled out the backdoor, still wearing the jacket & dress, giggling as they stumbled in their fancy clothes. Wide stripy cuffs flapped on Sam's arms. Jimi sailed along the wet pavement, his pearl train glowing in the twilight.

Waiting for the Sibyl
after Abbas Kiarostami

Eight to four, I sat in a purple courtyard. Tomorrow, I was told, maybe tomorrow. I never saw the sibyl, crashing my assignment, had no byline to peddle, no proof for the doubters, another Abel wandering the world with a mark against him. For years I've studied the shadows that lurk behind a curtain, listening for a voice in the rafters. Visions flood my limbs before sleep churns like a pound lock, the sibyl ever mum, eyes spinning in the glass. I've made it my life's work to put words in her mouth.

My Unfinished Opera

I gas-painted my middle C & set the selfish ♪ on fire. Key of the hero, key of the ageing juggernaut, voices blazing under a satellite dome. I could stake my vision, but I couldn't snatch the mood, paste the crescendo to the metronome. My opera demanded a silent finale. It was agreed: my silent, unfinished opera. I loaded an aria, two serenades, three concertinos in the clean cartridge. Like any great lover, I was born to spin that singing wheel. The world was at one, this would be a masterpiece.

Interdependence Day
July 4

My maternal grandfather, born in 1896, & who didn't know
rock & roll from a Christmas carol, framed the paper,
that loud black headline blaring from his office wall:
Elvis Pressley Is Dead. A Mizrahi Jew who fled Europe
with his wife & kids in '38, he clocked for the rations board,
basking in that blue-chip fountain,
the stock market of the 1960s.
My grandparents didn't own any of Elvis's albums;
their music collection consisted of a single LP,
Nina Simone's debut, a gift from one of their kids
that probably seemed appropriate,
given that Simone grew up in Tryon,
the same town where they lived,
albeit on the other side of the Catasheep River,
across train tracks, past the cop station,
in the gulley where flood waters pooled every time it rained.
Nina fled Tryon as soon as she could, wrapping
herself in a neon gown, overdosing on jazz chords.
She died by an open window
in a spaceship flying to the sun,
dreaming of one final concert,
an electric piano that floated in the dark.
My grandfather's sister died in a concentration camp in '44.
My mother says that most meals the ghost woman sat grimly at their table,
flashing her tattooed arm as often as she could.
Elvis ate fried food & took sleeping pills.
The last ten years of his life, he gained 180 pounds.
He was my grandfather's American son,
who tossed his hips for a Nashville moment
while in Tryon we waited in our trucks for the Northern Suffolk to pass.
Baptism, burial, a lifetime flashes
before that caboose finally arrives.
My grandfather, safe among the magnolia trees,
died on his back porch. 1980, roses in blossom,
heart bursting as he stared into a wisteria hedge.

You could almost hear Nina's jazz chords writhing in the grass.
Steam coiled above the Catasheep River. The Northern Suffolk
carved across the mountainside. A month
after his service, I helped my grandmother pack boxes.
"He adored The King," she said, glancing at the '77 headline,
& I figure that on some level what she said had to be true,
though I don't think my grandfather could've named one Elvis song
if his sister's life depended on it. & it probably did.

No Longer July

Sometimes it jumbles,
beats from a K-pop project,
Stefan's poem about the coordinates of war.
Detective Ana Garcia's voicemail
splits the airwaves, how she unscrewed the door from its hinges,
boring her flashlight into a curtained room
—Richard slumped in his chair,
a scarecrow with a postcard lacquered to his chest.
Now I rescan the email from his ex,
insisting that she loved him
despite the way their short summer ended.
Regardless of who loved who or didn't, it's been a year
since I swore off arguing with the dead.
The things we carry: how it's never enough
to stand shirtless in a field, singing the truth,
you need someone across the fence to applaud, to say yes,
you were there when the gun went off, though you weren't.
Yeah, you reached for the barrel at the last moment,
though you were five hundred miles away,
rummaging through bills
or changing a light bulb
or trying to get to the bottom of why
your newspaper wasn't delivered.
I wish I could tell her that if she weeps long enough, he'll return,
floating above her king-sized bed at 3AM,
mouthing *all is forgiven baby*,
but even he can't chase away that reek of sulfur,
it's all yours, it hovers, thick as
guilt or longing or resentment,
until you don't need it anymore, you roar
in the middle of the night it's gone.

The Music at Hand

I saw the news about the famous drummer found
pulseless in his hotel room in Bogotá, the boulevard
outside the Casa Medina lined with sunflowers,
fans singing through the night. Truth is, I didn't know
much about him, & I flashed on my old friend Richard,
how we used to chop lines of speed in his garage,
Richard pounding those flea-market Ludwigs as I
banged on my knock-off Gibson, slobbering into a
Radio Shack microphone. We scored one gig, opening
for his brother's girlfriend, fifteen minutes under a
purple disco ball. Richard was fast, slow, no one cared,
least of all me, floating in feedback, kicking bottles
off the stage. Years later, I spent a month whispering
to myself in a basement before nurses doused my skull
with current, lightning sloshed in my brain, so many
pages devoured. I ascended, stumbling back to the
bright platform of the living, that synaptic chorus
dredged from a muddy tomb. Now I pause, listening
to the famous drummer drum, a playlist that unfurls
like a long memento mori, an extended adagio clipped
into FM flares. I try to recall Richard's face, his sarcasm,
they're verses I can't quite conjure, refrains that
elude me. His brother called in 2012, it was late March
then too, the suburban yards shimmered with daffodils,
lavender blooms. Richard had died from an overdose,
found by neighbors face-down on a shag carpet, his dog
barking over his corpse. So many dead by needle, pills,
in fiery wrecks, souls who refused to succumb to the
tempo life demanded, drummers who flogged the beat
until no one could find it or lagged until the song fell apart.
Today my city's young again with the rhythms of spring,
but I'm spelled by ghosts, they huddle in the shadows,
voices slurring on repeat, as if begging to be heard.
& I hear them, at least for a few measures, before I turn away,
shoving myself sunward, back to the music at hand.

Resurrection Day
for Greg

That Easter, my godmother took me to the tent revival.
Look John, she said, can you see the diamonds in the sky?
I said I could, & after the preacher roared his sermon,
we rushed the altar to be healed.
Ms. Caroline gripped me by the wrist.
I dove down Jesus's hot white throat
as a man in the front row
thrashed in the dirt, Ms. Caroline
hurling her eyes cloud-ward.
How I yearned to see the angels above me, to hear
that stone rolling from the grave. Later
we drove while the radio played salvation tunes.
Ms. Caroline ground her teeth,
that silver cross dangling from her rear-view mirror.
        My brother-in-law died today,
Resurrection Sunday. For years, he proclaimed the word,
voice messages that brimmed with New Testament quotes,
yarns about a raging hunger,
how he dropped to his knees in a black river,
& when he rose, there was no place he couldn't call home.
        Children comb the branches of trees,
peer under rocks, sprawl in flowerbeds.
They smear Jesus's black pulp across their mouths,
reenacting the revels of our fairytale fathers,
who stabbed & ripped the old gods' flesh,
roused the new gods from their burbly slumber,
singing & stomping to an ageless beat.
        You shall press the hammer to your brow, I was told,
& know the agony of the universe.
You shall soar with wings on loan from the emperor of light.
A thousand graves empty in the radiant spring.
Shadows dissolve in the grass,
land of pollen & wafting blooms.
These decades worn, I see that congregation, eyes

aglow, hands clutching the ankles of the Lord.
He is risen, Ms. Caroline said,
our sorrow his love shall fire to ash.
I press my palms to my ears to mute that
terrifying hallelujah, it echoes in the long, red field.

Gospel/Amethyst County

The heavenchase is won by the dream mare,
who spits the bit, hoofing in the wet night.
I could be the unsaddled mustang flying through dawn,
carrying the messenger
back to the house where he started,
the house of apocalypse,
windowless church where a blind choir
sings its brittle hymn
over & over to the vacant pews.
I could kick forever in the sunlight, my rider
dead—but still talking—from three silver bullets.

Ode to Impermanence

anatta

I tossed in the glare, thumbing a lever
until the nurse shoved me an Oxy in a paper cup.
Hot, hungry, rolling from one dream
to another. But who dreamed? Who
unraveled that white thread, grazing
the catastrophes of mind & body?
Electrodes glued to my skin,
I dreamt of a rattlesnake coiled in my bed.
I dreamt of our father, who threw open
a second-story window, jabbing a shotgun
into the green breast of an oak tree.
Johnny he said *bring me that tombird.*
I went looking for it, barking in the mulch,
sniffing that mound of butterfly wings.
I couldn't find it, when I turned back our father was gone.
I woke & yelled his name, the morning
was a warm chandelier crashing to the floor.

Remembering Richard

I scored a gig with a photographer named Richard, hours
on a site outside Sedona, my job to cart his lights & tripods,
rusty implements of the trade, gadgetry amassed over decades.
I didn't love being cooped up in a New Age-y villa, staging
antique furniture, the standing around, waiting & waiting.
But the pay was good, & when the sun spilled through a west-
facing window, the world a prehistoric red, we packed & Richard
got us a cab into the city. *You know we have numerous lives,*
he said over a martini, telling me of his theater days in Berkeley,
apprenticeship to a moody auteur in the channels off Gothenburg,
his twenty-eighth birthday spent filming the sadhus of Varanasi.
I lived to fall in love, he added, describing the mad novelist
he wooed in Barcelona, a barista from Warsaw, his plunge
into the matrix of the flesh, a vampiric genius from Tangier
branding him with a spell that took a stale year to overcome.
How 'bout you? he asked. *Not much to say,* I blurted, a blank
screen dropping, my mouth suddenly dry. *Not yet!* he quipped,
leaping into a mazy anecdote about a chess match he lost in Berlin.
He spoke of Shakespeare, Socrates, the Aztecs & Incas. We ate
spicy cornbread, guzzled beer & shots of gin. Richard scaled
his monologues, a speed-climber ascending a mountain peak,
diving into a boundless fog, that elastic pause. Finally we rode
back to the Louis Hotel, Richard stumbled to his suite, mumbling
in French. I found my room & dropped into a carnival of sleep.
Three women sang a dirge while I swung a pickaxe in a desert,
a vision that returned when my mother died, again when I
quit drinking, years later following a friend's suicide, three women
cringing as I buried a blade in the ancient sand. I crank the bright
umber of Richard's eyes, can summon the music of his voice,
though I'm sure he's deceased by now, a severed cord flapping
in the stratosphere. I wake & slumber & wake again, haunted
by the fact that some capricious dawn the waking simply ends,
who can say if there's another dream on the other side of this one.

Bonson County
for BW, mid-80s

I wrestled the Pawtalaskee Bridge, hoisted at dawn, lowered at dusk.
Between, soaked my canvases, stab of onyx, slice of crimson,
the flood in the baffled vein. Watercolor nodding.
So it went, into the wood-burning winter when there
was no wood, no cash, & the Soho gallery stopped calling,
last drip of paint dabbed from the mangled soda can.
The river turned blue, the bridge in lockjaw.
I sold my grandmother's quilts, gold, fifty silver dollars.
I lived like that for three months, shaking in the monster's arms.

Cold

for DW

Hours before the dogs plowed the ivy,
dragging loud summer in their teeth,
I'd been transposed mid-refrain,
bass clef branded on my inner thigh.
He glued a bow into my left hand,
tearing arpeggios from the moon.
I was his sculpture, tableau, diorama,
his failed baptism turned inside out,
my intestines rang like singing bowls.
Cathedral constructed, tablature traced,
he paused in the ironweed, eyes skyward,
stamped his palms into the riverbed
as chains of new light shimmered on the hill.
He twined my last words around his lips,
tuned my spine, skin glowing with rosin,
tongue stretched like a whole note.
My flesh was the cello, cracked violin,
the babbling viola of his dreams,
his masterpiece wrenched from silence.

Conjugal
for KP

If you haven't figured it out yet,
this is a portrait of the man you married,
who hovered above his own body,
clutching his invisible horn. After
words & blurbs & the ash-house,
you found his favorite fanfares under the
couch cushion, the living-room carpet.
You swept them up, boiled them,
pinned them to a corkboard for safekeeping.
Next day, you heard mad wings
fluttering on the other side of the house.
Is that you? you said, tossing the sheets,
bolting toward that power flash. & he
staggered, as if at the end of a hallway,
dashing notes on your backsplash,
unspooling his crescendo as the sun rose.
You married an invisible man with an invisible horn.
You waited for him to find his body,
find his music, you doused him with arias.
You danced in your gown beside a window
as he floated in the rafters. Slapping
his invisible horn, he buckled
on his bad leg, tangled, stranded in that
hallway, lost between jilted rooms.

He was strung by his father, tuned
by his mother. He won a contest
when he was a boy, it shoved him into cold chairs,
a measure he never found his way out of.
His horn fell asleep in its case.
He slapped it & slapped it, it never woke.
He was a boy, the wrong people whispering in his ear,
a boy who heard the music calling, it sounded like a
stranger being abducted in a van, the scream
growing fainter until the van was gone,

76

the scream was gone, he played his winning refrain
on his invisible horn for his imaginary fans
while his cravings dilated in a minor key.
He blew & blew into his invisible horn,
asking you to carry the music he couldn't wake,
to applaud him, lost in a hallway.

You said you could feel him
clanging between molecules,
you could hear him more glaringly
than when he stammered barefoot through the kitchen,
dragging his solo behind him.
He was married to you, but he
borrowed his timbre from another muse,
leashed himself across the floor,
that shuffle by the hutch & the liquor bin.
He fiddled with knobs on the stove,
sorrow reeking of poppies & garlic,
hurled steak knives & a grater into the microwave.
He smashed a vase, stamped a riff on the tan carpet,
an inky coda on the kitchen wall.
One neighbor said: *it sounded like a snare drum.*
Another neighbor said: *it sounded like a muffled bell.*
He was married to you, he stood
in a hallway, hands wrapped in gauze.
He played an invisible horn as bullheaded light
crashed through an open window.
Your phone kept ringing no matter
how many times you answered it,
the great fires began to burn.

Two Years 2

You treaded all summer in the blackberry heat
while I lowered myself into the drain,
fiddling with my headlamp,
calling to you in that heroin quarry.
Stethoscope, Narcan, defibrillator,
the paramedic's fingers stapled to your wrist.
Now it's winter, hard to believe
I'm pounding chords on your baby grand,
two years & what comes home
to me every time is silence, & then more silence.

Lead

I drove a flatbed in Nelson's Lair,
looking for marbles, shine, the kind of saw
you bend into a song over bad coffee
& a blowtorch. You could call it selective
memory, the lull of aftermath,
but there was a nation of ice
between me & the free road.
A Jungian would have a field day with this.
A purist would say *sit until you disappear.*
I poured smoke into my throat,
I fled downriver, floating in my father's rafters.
I begged St. Monica & the stars,
years lost in the Lower Burrows, a hand
plucked me from the thick white line,
the pipe & chasing glass.
In the beginning, I learned a safeword,
it's taken me a long time to use it.

Crossroads

We stumbled between trees, young & drunk,
hollers from home, convinced
the devil would emerge,
extending his hand, our tickets to immortality.
He never showed, & I'd wake, stormy-headed, Richard gone,
or I'd wake, Richard sprawled in the leaves,
cum on his pants, & I'd leave him there,
embarrassed to be my brother's keeper.
Years later & for decades,
I ignored a voice faint but steadfast,
inconsequence hovering in boardrooms,
over million-dollar budgets & white-crowded tables,
that mix of vanity & discontent.
Richard married & divorced three times,
stalked a teacher in Memphis.
He was last seen barefoot in the snow,
curling a screwdriver outside a duplex in Birmingham.
These memories blast through me,
current that shakes me in my boots,
a sporadic throb on loan. Nothing coheres,
details floating in weightless air, restless void.
There are secrets I was born to tell,
though I've lacked the heart to speak
or failed to convert that fire into words. Plus, no one
wants to hear about the last fair deal gone down,
how it was crooked from the get-go, this invisibility
I've spent a lifetime trying to deny, it reminds me
of chasing shadows in the morning.

Adventures in Real Estate

We swapped ditties in my parents' kitchen,
my 12-string Yamaha, your father's ukulele,
while upstairs the grad student whittled her thesis,
shouting profanity at a computer screen.
I wanted you to spend the night,
I wanted to climb inside you & never come out,
shiny amor unspooling like radio jazz.
I could've lived my life that way,
one helluva day after another.
You tweaked a phrase, I teased a melody,
I haven't seen you since we were teenagers
splashing in pop tunes & pentatonic scales.
But then, this story brims with surrogates & impossible desire,
a chance to be saved on my own terms.
Our choruses fluttered into silence,
the mourning dove that nested in my mother's throat
still cooing in the tall grass,
& the grad student long gone,
a copy of her thesis stashed in the attic,
buried beneath mannequins & a cracked guitar.
Wind blows through an open window.
Wind blows through a cluttered room.
This is a happy ending.

Tableau Vivant

You shrank all summer,
palms pressed to the window,
flowerpots rooted to the floor.
You snatched the 22 from ether,
sprouting those gunpowder wings.
Urgency is masked by calm,
dour resolve like a fishtail palm
dropping its seed before it wilts,
a final hurrah. You
burned a manuscript, you
deleted the files on your laptop,
a disappearing act
performed while no one was watching.
I have your smoky props,
I have the photos, the what-ifs,
I have that last conversation
& these crawling hours
to parse what was said
& what wasn't.

Impermanence
for Thia

Richie finally gets his '69 Corvette,
cruises uptown Bardo with big cash,
shredding solos for his mentor, treating
the cheerleaders to hotdogs & beer.
I text the ferryman & convince him
to skip our port, lassoing the goodbye sun.
Richie idles on a boomerang curve,
honking for me to join him. Those
last days of summer, that teenage Gethsemane,
frayed my wiring. These decades later,
I flicker in doorways, at thresholds,
battlegrounds where the sidewalk ends
& the rest of your life begins.
Richie goads his Corvette, plows that
diamond ramp, launching into the twilight.
Of course the ferry arrives.
You lean over the balcony, tangled
in rainbow vines, waving to me.
A terrible wind blows, & I page back
to the rough water. When the anchor drops,
I want to run for the bluffs, steal another day,
another shimmering chorus, but my feet
are frozen, & night crashes on the shore.

Acknowledgments

The poet thanks the editors of the following publications, in which many of these poems previously appeared.

2River View: "To Find You Like That"
American Literary Review: "Legacy"
Anti-Heroin Chic: "Catherine," "Two Years 2"
Constellate: "Pivot"
Cultural Daily: "Family Systems," "Regrets," "Two Years," "Conjugal"
FEED: "Bonson County," "First Marriage"
Frigg: "Breathless," "Haunted," "Foster"
Ghost City Press: "Ode to Impermanence"
Glint: "What I Remember"
great weather for MEDIA: "Remembering Richard," "Days of Love & Horses," "Understudy"
Hoxie Gorge: "Arc"
Into the Void: "Where the Work Is"
Jam & Sand: "First Date," "Fifteen"
Long Islander: "Multiverse"
Maryland Literary Review: "Apprenticeship"
Menacing Hedge: "A Funeral Dream," "Cold"
Modern Poetry Quarterly: "The 49 Days"
New York Quarterly: "Crossroads," "The Music at Hand," "Resurrection Day," "Poem for Bill B"
North Carolina Bards Against Hunger: "Addict," "Gospel/Amethyst County"
Offcourse: "Anniversary 2," "Bardo," "At Some Point," "Vigil," "Waiting for the Sibyl"
One: "Impermanence"
ONE ART: "The 80s"
Paterson Literary Review: "Tableau Vivant," "Defiance"
Poetrybay: "Adventures in Real Estate"
Prairie Schooner: "Relapse," "Recovery"
Prism: "Toward a Genealogy"
Rattle: "Interdependence Day"

RHINO: "Local News"

Rust + Moth: "Souvenirs," "After Your Memorial," "Roman à Clef,"
  "Dark Souvenirs"

SOLO: "Lead"

Spillway: "Homecoming"

SurVision: "Backstory," "My Unfinished Opera," "Ode to Country
  Music," "Ode to Country Music 2," "Ode to Mythology"

West Trade Review: "Usually when I recall you"

"No Longer July" was the recipient of the 2021 Jack Grapes Poetry
Prize and was published in October 2021 by *Cultural Daily*

John Amen is the author of five collections of poetry, including *Illusion of an Overwhelm* (NYQ Books), finalist for the 2018 Brockman-Campbell Award, and work from which was chosen as a finalist for the 2018 Dana Award. He was the recipient of the 2021 Jack Grapes Poetry Prize, and his poems have been translated into Spanish, French, Hungarian, Korean, and Hebrew. He founded and is managing editor of *Pedestal Magazine*. His music, literary, and film reviews appear regularly in various publications. He has studied the Enneagram extensively and is a certified teacher in the Narrative Enneagram Professional Training Program. He lives with his wife—artist, designer, and Dharma leader Thia Powers.

Printed in the USA
CPSIA information can be obtained
at www.ICGtesting.com
JSHW072018250324
59905JS00013B/56